Lifestyle
of a god in my
Brothers' eyes

Cornelius Joseph

SWEETSPIRE **LITERATURE**
—— MANAGEMENT ——

TABLE OF CONTENTS

Acknowledgements. v

Introduction. vii

Chapter I. Lifestyle: 1

Chapter II. god: 8

Chapter III. BROTHERS' 17

Chapter IV. Eyes 23

Biography. 25

ACKNOWLEDGEMENTS

Please write your acknowledgement here . . . I hope that this book help encourage those who feel lost. By establishing a beacon of hope, no matter what struggle or condition that lays ahead throughout life itself. We as an American people must find ourselves by learning from those past lives whom witnessed such enormous strides, however gaining acceptance in part by taking responsibility for future generational accomplishments. I do not wish to impose any value system, yet open minds and make sure the human family grasp a connection or concept of the world that's susceptible for change through character. May God himself bless you in every aspect that makes life beautiful and worth living.

INTRODUCTION

Please give a short intro of the story here ……

Lifestyle of a god in my Brothers' eyes portray a journey within a thrall condition that outlays the painful truth. The journey is finding oneself in comparison with chronological worldly event's, by seeing life through different eyes, to serve as a window to the soul. The search for Renaissance, through a turbulent lifestyle, to achieving prominence. A quick and powerful epic read that exposes a conscientious point of view towards a realistic vicious cycle.

Lifestyle of a god in my Brothers' eyes is a bildungsroman spiritual awakening of a person within the social inner city experiences of the American ghetto in relation to classes of American society. All classes in America share the same English speaking cultures, but in regards toward traditions, social norms, and economic upheavals may vary within a systematic structure according to ideology and diversity. To my knowledge, there exist many classes in America. The upper class, middle class, lower class, and a waste of last class. The educational, religious, cultural, and working classes were considered the upper and middle classes. These classes extended from the east coast to the west coast, along the Great Lakes, down the Mississippi River, into the Gulf of Mexico; (Manifest Destination).

The dramatic changes that are relevant in today's society compel the struggles of an American people past and present. The book also focuses on a renaissance in communities thrall by corruption within a system of immorality. For example, the ghetto becoming a slum is a direct result from decades of corruption and criminal activity causing systematic oppressions by practicing an unlawful lifestyle of mismanagement of ethical ethos, damaged by distractions of free will; the trappings of today's young adults and youths becoming criminals.

God, in my Brothers' eyes mentions a theory of history repeating itself in scripture. By understanding what motivates, definitely drive a society to thrive by defying or improving the system with greatness, or be lost with its people's failures for generations. The bildungsroman is the moral and psychological growth of an individual faced with adversity and seeing life from the perspective of pioneers which are consistent means to cultural exchanges, reluctantly lasting throughout the ages.

Men, such as Andrew Carnegie, John D. Rockefeller, J.P. Morgan, and Henry Ford established the world of industry. These men, whom rarely had much time to talk of their struggles or misfortunes because of such sacrifices in industrial expansion. The harsh reality of industry were working conditions, with low wages, exploitation of labor over time, left a rift and placed a burden in the hands of responsible women to carry the family or the load. A result form of less trickle-down economics occurred in the poor working classes over competition in labor, pay, and working conditions. As men would build cities while women cared for dependents in the days of the Industrial Revolution.

The post industrial age is different, an ongoing process, but has repeating similarities. Men worked while women raised children of the future, bringing about Women's rights along with the 20th century imaginary movements. We are all part of an American value system woven together by a fabric of cultures from migrating immigrants, compelled to progress in pursuit of the 'American Dream' taught throughout American society. Everyone has a choice inside their community. Historians lifestyles were based on choices and facts giving way as the soulful purpose to individuals; an intuitive view of American values taken in regards toward society the needs for prosperity.

Everyday people are lawful citizens who vote to help establish and adopt new laws in dealing with crimes against humanity, but the uneducated and lack of charitable training rarely got recognized, which was an area I chose to make a study of the weaknesses. The difficulties of the underemployed, working poor and downtrodden were discrimination, black on black crimes resulting from social injustice led by a bribery, robbery, rioting, looting, selling of illegal drugs, to abuse of women, and senseless deaths, also for those lacking political and social consciousness. In relation to the American Justice System and criminal justice system, the dealings of unjustified force by applying more pressure as a result to the combating powers that opposes such threats of domesticated crimes along with international implications.

According to street life, the crime bill imposed on felons established an inferiority or illiteracy complex. These conspiracy theories were welcomed in an environment intertwined by ethnicity and or genders promoting illegal activity. A grim reality resulted, whereby the str8, L, B, G, T, Q, communities became rivals in a society divided amongst property owners, politicians, ministers, and law enforcement. These conspiracy theories of organize chaos materialized as a peculiar language emerged amongst different ethnic backgrounds, whereby fueling illegal activity, such as drug trafficking, thievery, prostitution, and conspiracy. Not only domestic violence was of the times, but many of the laws ran parallel with domestic terrorism, affecting those who were politically unaware, and "if you didn't relate to them, the systematic power structure would organize them against you." [Bobby Seal, Seize The Time].

Separate but equal; you can knock it down, but can't knock it out. Therefore, educating communities for endowed mental objectives and creating diversity were vital in moving forward. So, by speaking universal conventional wisdom to the most productive of people that can acquire human, social, and financial capital, an important endeavor in all aspects in relations to familial and societal life.

The plan is to replace marginalization of blacks with a form of self help or a societal economic structuring that's beneficial as a whole. Do to urban sprawl, urban placement, and urban decay thwarted any perseverance for any advancements as I observed the rampart activity bargaining down the Black community.

If there ever were to be any message of communications allowed to spread amongst Brothers' from multiple backgrounds, it'll have to be a miracle of divine intervention. I believe I'm living and witnessing five worlds integrated by Red, White, Black, Yellow, and colored people's throughout America. I had to be strong like the well educated previous predecessors whom instilled principles in the past centuries to present times. The most influential people, such as Dolly Madison, Abe Lincoln to the likes of Eleanor Roosevelt, Paul Robeson, Mohandas Gandhi, and Dr. Martin Luther King Jr. The Coded Colors consistent with spirituality, ethics, and morality which are liberties granted in a Democracy.

I am an African Native American with an Eurasian complexity, which are the Codes of many Colors (Lost tribe of Joseph), due to the perplexity of the American society. By concentrating and using my literary knowledge in English, a narrative perspective into the eight parts of speech serving as a guide. When speaking English, take linguistics, syntax, and semantics. The English language can be spoken in terms of order in comparison to regional dialects, singing, speech, acting, and debate. I consider four hypothesis. The language of order, the language of low order, the language out of order, and the language under order or orders.

CHAPTER I. LIFESTYLE:

Growing up here in East St. Louis, Illinois had its strongest points recollected in my mind. It wasn't so much emphasis on thinking, but being brought up and guided in the ways of the living. What was seldom seen I observed quite cautiously, whether unified, separated, and or departed. It seemed that the Elders were moving towards a higher power or spiritual entity for an awakening, where as the younger generation were trying to find their place of identity in the world. This had intrigue. Although my experience as a young man levitated towards the elders, yet I remained immersed amongst the company of my peers. I noticed a gap in generations fleeced by occurrences amongst families and friends bound to becoming enemies. Many were rebellious, afraid, frustrated and instilled within the bitter moments of segregation and Jim Crow during 50's and 60's. They went through hell, but the times were changing as the elders were well condition for the struggles.

By distancing myself to better understand and get a grasp of this anomaly, voiced by an individual's concern, but in silence. I was on a quest. It was quite revealing and rooted deeply in American culture. The culture was shifting and this audio synchronization of art became the norm. Rap music had its own cultural influences unlike blues and jazz. The content became negative and materialized into common life. In today's society, the common man would be considered a peon. Everything seemed gangsta', which caught us by surprise. The potency of lyrical content adding a bass line with musical melody, along with subliminal images capable of reaching the masses, whether pleasant or distasteful. The precursor to present day social media. My intuition, perhaps one of the most important ability I knew at that time, resembled the wisdom of the ancestors that made me feel as if I was a minor god.

By casting myself as a minor god into the lifestyle from whence thy came as a personal studier into the many philosophical principles of the post Mecca Malcolm X and training of Bruce Lee. In loving memory and guidance embraced by a spiritual Red Indian. My primordial homeland of Monks Mounds where I pray is located at Cahokia Mounds between Collinsville and East St. Louis, Illinois. My intent was to acquire a spiritual connection and allow wisdom with the resources to gain an understanding in finding an intellectual view providing a solution, to compose a world picture and place renaissance in this world sector. I chose my hometown of East St. Louis, Illinois.

In late October, during autumn of 1993, the weather was cool and gloomy in East St. Louis, Illinois as I stood outside my mother's house. While standing, I had many thoughts going on in my mind about unemployment. Apathy started setting in the community and conditions were getting even worse; frustrations definitely didn't make it better, either. It was getting late for some of the homies who were smoking weed. There were a dozen of us at the time. Many were ordinary guys who didn't cause trouble, since our hood was well known for its reputation, we generally kept to ourselves. We were of age whereby we had grown up. Needless to say, we all were innocent in society at the time. The smallest yet most knowledgeable, I generally held discussions about trying to be productive by staying straight and embarking upon a community endeavor. Some of us who avoided temptation of the street life, somehow figured it was bound to catch up with us. It wasn't me though, from looking back, I was well aware to refrain from such temptations.

Every day the same thing concerning domestic violence happening near home was always bad. There was nothing new about street life that didn't surprise us. We figured that we were a generation destined for something, but deep inside we had the biggest strike against us. We were young black men. A bunch of field 'niggas' with no definite direction on where we were headed. As we passed the blunt around taking turns puffing on it and sometimes uttering gestures of jokes just to get laughs, therefore just having fun. Somehow, we were perceived in our hood as hoodlums, outcasts, and a waste of last class. It's too difficult for us to think that way because it was all good. It's a damn shame being watched by individuals that were either jealous or just didn't take liking to us for no apparent reason because of their own ignorance. This judgment became a dagger to my Black race. From past experiences, I noticed those with there asses so high on their shoulders, to even help one another would upset the Great divide of the colored line. These division towards one another rival the very essence of being black men. This was more deadly than racism.

Their own black culture denied them the opportunity to branch out and see life in the eyes of others. Dreams seemed to be overshadowed by nightmares for a town breeding warfare, consequently in a place where no one played fair while heading to nowhere. The difference between a bad ass child in comparison to a spoil ass child. This distinction is the most troublesome of the black male. The truth of the matter is one thinks he can get himself out of trouble and the other taking his parents through turmoil to bail us out. What do these negroes expect? A voice from the past sounding like an echo sending a message of an inheritance not yet dead. Whispering, "the white man, we are hear!" We all knew this was a lie, as time passed, we realize time over end it never came, so we decided to go our separate paths towards our own existence, to seek the possibility of truth for our own benefits or beliefs. There was a moment of silence with libation, then we went home.

We were like that of the 'Roaring twenties'. As young adults, we were very aware of the changing times. Normally doing the same things every weekend which was making some money working low paying jobs, gambling, playing sandlot and street basketball. Riding around in cars to meet up for sporting events while listening to loud underground hip-hop, and rock-n-roll, as music consumed the parkway wherever we played. In moderation we drank alcohol, smoked weed and chased after women. Attending night club events where dancing also was a major part of cultural aspirations during the times. As I looked, I saw a crowd astonished by surprised that I was unaware of, but I thought and I look as if it wasn't nothing, period. It seemed mesmerizing by this nostalgia, but in Life, it was only a mirage. The flesh is just feelings that goes nowhere, but to dust, and my spirit is everlasting.

The karma from this lifestyle resulted in creativity, whereby telling the times when I was at my best potential. In all my essence, I discovered myself in writing, dance, art, and work ethics. I told everybody, "witness god in my flesh," as I was attracted to mostly all cultures in regards to music for dance. Not discrediting anyone, as for as the sweet pleasures of youth were concern, but we had to focus and pertain energy to reviving cultural art diversity in a vibrant city. Such as the likes of Katherine Dunham, Tina Turner, and Miles Davis. They were iconic in music and dance. Home is special. I sat back nonchalantly to reminisce, occasionally listening to everyone; some were quiet and others were just chillin' out. I had this interest in writing dance art because the talent possess a potential for mediate neighborhood responses, for those of us who had a hell of a lot of street knowledge that added to the culture.

There were those who were power hungry, but didn't quite know how to go about it. I often wondered how to get them not to play the big man roll, because that way of control would yield casualties from judging the negative substance abusive activities running rampart in the metropolitan area. If I could seize their attitudes from them by channeling it towards a business oriented perspective, then acknowledging them wouldn't be of any problems. I reiterated that I don't want to be the boss, only the initiator of what should happen towards our survival. The necessary thing to do, by all means. For one moment corruption cannot come amongst us.

We start together, therefore we finish together. Because of society, I'm compelled to believe that thought would come up again, but in a later time. There were a lot of people to mention, but I tried to reach the men and women in my community, first. I also tried to organize a private meeting and we all can discuss the arts to one another and later to group performances. By the meeting being circumstantial, we would have to move with alacrity if we wanted to make it look good. Our organization has to be established within a few months.

Working slowly adds more cooperation. There were those who were opportunistic and would thwart progress. That's why I designed an ancient system I adopted from the Native Americans (Circle of Life). By designing this specific way of (Rise to Balance) (my) life. The signifying art wouldn't refer back to a head-man. The Son of the Sun all ways rises in the east and sets in the west as my representation of the giver of life.

I recalled a notion of heaven's feet dancing in the sunlight amongst the motion of the western winds. To be correct, no one should be accused of believing in my talents. Quite actually, the precedent would just go in circles to find the return of a so called, Omnipotent Leader. By journeying to the one place where it all originated with a Native American prayer to all my relations, my ancestors clasp- in hands of prayer. I journeyed to Monks Mounds and I prayed. I asked, Christ±Kwagalta (an unbeknown King of my 500 nations), I came to make an offering by circumventing the 'America Dream' indeterminately.

By utilizing Mendel's Law of Independent Assortment. A dedicated service for the future of humanity. Also, rediscovering a renaissance in America and introducing a phenomenal principle of occurrences. Art transforms life. An universal expression of dancing illustrates future work ethics regarding writing towards humane libertarian curriculums, sighted by individuals during special moments on a celestial projections; the unexplainable. So, when people get a glimpse of an ancestral Dance Master resembling 'ghostly' rhythmic patterns, their memories are coded to a healthy human being aligned with the twelve tribes. Afterword's, I returned home.

Society yielded opposition and that's why I was out here like a seed acquiring hope. As a child, I remembered as I stood in the sunlight-rays shining through the windows of our home. God created sun light. The one source I need to take along my journey, burning internally to remain free. What haven't I learned, as I sat down facing the setting sun on my mother's porch reminiscing about solving the current situations. For one, I nearly was broke, two, seasonal employment, Three, damn near homeless, and helping women support their children with what little I had to offer at the time. Working construction and building maintenance jobs fueled my mediate lifestyle.

I got up and search the ground to find a history of children school assignments that may never be found. An ongoing process that currently exists in my home town. A humanitarian prophet who considered myself with them, but always seeing myself caring as if I was helpless to her beckon calls. An attractive beauty far beyond measures of control. I felt chosen for a limited time to share comfort that has always been with me mysteriously.

Reminding myself that true romance took my mind away from the negativity of street life by imagining mother and child. I thought about the creators blessings. I didn't have children of my own, but vivid thoughts of my mother caring for me as a child without a father. My stay was brief and seeing them in good health was pleasing. I recalled Adam spending some time on Mother Earth. During that time, he reigned dominion over the angels until Eve came along. Although I felt this life was hard, I couldn't see a permanent commitment, therefore, I disregarded the thought due to grief and envy, so that she can Seek Inner-Self to Every Reason, Honor of our Dreams. I just had to remind myself that no one man can know it all, but only enough to protect one's well being if fortunate and quite intuitive about his surroundings.

As I await the perfect moment to begin the work I dedicated myself was no longer with me, but this harem I noticed that eased tensions, and I found myself being hard on myself and not worthy of a life I lacked, due to chasing the 'American Dream' caused me to run away. Being a product of this instance was perhaps the failures of my father's plagued DNA, but often I witnessed God in my flesh on Monks Mound where I prayed. Settling down may have became my greatest challenge, because people were too quick to forget the pursuit of happiness, instead participate in the full swing of an American Dream of insecurities.

Personally, I believe some people should abstain from family life for a while, until he or she comes of age. Because it will be difficult to raise monks and virgins in a community overwhelmed by the temptation of sensuality for subliminal images and messages meant as a distraction inserted into learning. Perhaps a journey or a Quest to educate and learn for thyself, if he or she's a soldier or in pursuit of perfection by his or her talents geared towards the 'American Dream'. I firmly believe the male must know himself first at his best potential in whatever area of education provided on the earth. A social/economic balance with spiritualism, and work ethics. Do to a strict upbringing, I never illustrated such emotions or passions for females until my college years where I began intermingling amongst a diverse groups. It was suggested by those who were closest to me and I thanked them very much. In my home town, I didn't have the time to concern myself with taboo. If there were any foreseeable future, I had to grow up, relearn an old family traditions, an inheritance of my grandmother's wisdom, to move forward from an athletic imbalance household changing into a substance abused, prescription retirement home.

My primary education was based on a Native American Red Indian, my grandmother Ethel, who believed I must remain a monk in educated pursuits, because once black males start having sex early in life, they'll lose focus for awhile becoming adversely woven into life's sweet pleasures. I noticed a lot of women and children faced with historical illiteracy in this life cycle. Nothing seems to last long in a broken home and I preferred to live alone. I caught glimpses of family members and friends gripped by low order. Family values was just another racist code term, meaning why that woman have three or four children and she ain't got no husband.

I felt it best not to participate in such a life. A true statement about good men are hard to find. One thing's for certain, with enough skills, one can find a niche. Construction jobs made me felt, I existed to help raise and build up a nation called The United States of America. Therefore, I swore to my grandmother, by remaining in the education that founded me and never shall I depart. The only way to stay strong was to live as the monk; I was conditioned and instructed to remain in the guidance of two Goddess Professors, whom are my soul mates and a Master of Heavenly Wisdom, forever. These three blessed souls were my most sacred; responsible for my greatness in writing, dance, art, and work ethics, I carry with me everywhere. I am called (Closest to God) by Lakota Sioux and (Nanne-Yah) by West African Zulu. I must keep God himself close to me. I had to learn and adopt from faiths in relation to a code of many colors called Ju'Christ'lam (Indigenous Hebrewism) Masha/Shalom.

To all my relations,

A man is not a nation

only a vessel of creation

Whom thirsts for libation

to conquer an end, with duration

of rights, to stand in ovation

Amongst a modern civilization

CHAPTER II. GOD:

Revelation 19:10 "And I fell at his feet to worship him. And he said unto me see thou do it not; I am thy fellow servant and thy bretheren that have the testimony of Jesus; worship God: for the testimony of Jesus is the spirit of prophecy." Revelation 19:12 "His eyes were as flame of fire and on his head were many crowns and he had a name written, that no man knew but himself." Some stated that the anti-Christ was coming from the east. I thought to myself, not East St. Louis. If that is so, then after witnessing the wrath of God's celestial order of angels, archangels, principalities, powers, virtues, dominions, thrones, cherubim, and seraphim to the heavens, the second coming of Jesus is taking Joseph along: Thou Will Shall Be Done. The savior's visionary compared to Eurion, seated at the East of God's Throne, within the belt of Orion, just over the horizon; where thy Kingdom come.

When I gazed into the eye of the sun, I actually saw an angel standing on the sun; my life was prophesied. I recalled my grandmother telling me only one time and I obeyed. I knew my family members led to my grandmother's demise and unaware of all the sickness and stress weakened our family structure. My crest, one of God's begotten daughters of Biblical interpretations. No one in the family had nothing good or bad to say about an elder. So, I was on my own seeking to dwell in the kingdom of heaven all by myself to manifest greatness. I had potential insight to see were my wrongs occurred. When I thought about it, it didn't make any difference if it was right or wrong. I am not a liar nor a fool: "the foolishness of God is wisest of all men."

Only a select few believed in my raw talents. There were many adverse people in the neighborhood, but they rarely understood my cross references of intelligentia. Unfortunately, they found it hard to figure and didn't seek to educate themselves. They lacked enthusiasm to come together during the greatest time since the history of the world. I foreshadowed the concept of a renaissance in my hometown disappear before my eyes. The support in the community never came, especially from family members and friends making unacceptable excuses and notions of premeditation for selfish gains. I never in my life participated in the hate that hate produces from self-destruction. I excommunicated myself for my work in creating (edutainmentelligence); spending considerable amounts of time privately, training, and researching information vital to my future. I saw no one with the same iconic interests as I, therefore I planned my departure to leave this place. No matter what threat or danger may have been posed on me, I never left as the enemy.

Setting out and embarking upon a sacred journey of truth for a raw talent, I floundered like an independent free thinker playing political football, as if it was a handheld game. I never played or joked around with them. I may share a laugh or two with them, but getting close was not an acceptance within myself. Even though I was civil, there were numerous attempts on my life by shenanigans posing as friends and disassembled family members forayed with drugs and guns to put me out, keep me out, maybe take me out even, whereby abandoned and forgotten about. Subsequently, I fled many times to save my life; (c.y.o.a) cover your on ass, only returning when it was safe.

My God given talents in writing, dance, art, and work ethics were electronically connected towards this American society as an informational grid for self- preservation. What actions can be taken for being a modeled law biding citizen? For years, I couldn't focus on my work, because I had to watch my back, then precede with caution. I quickly realized what can I do? I had little money. No type of authority or position of power to control anything, not even my own destiny, yet I had ambition. A stigma between those that lost interest and abandoning my talents had shifted their intentions toward the negative vices that plagued the community, even to this very day. Malcolm X, called it, "the trappings of the vicious cycle of apathy, ignorance, poverty, drugs, disease, and death."

The nigger garden mislead the nigger kingdom into being buried from nightmares that never woke them up. The mark of the beast with death, hell, and destruction at the helm. There were even those who were generations younger trying, or were tempting; too preoccupied by false pretenses, otherwise a limited vocabulary. I half-way listened to the people that couldn't see no further than their noses; in other words, treated them with a long handled spoon.

Therefore, God and time is on my side which transformed me beyond their scope of keeping up with compassionate intelligence, with the ability of spiritual dance phenomenon. The forewarnings of threatening conversations emerged in households throughout the city. Instead of 'Armageddon creativity', senseless deaths plagued the community while others planned their escape from those areas who lost track of themselves. Many took up arms as drugs and money became the reality. I had to remain alone because every participant were considered adversaries with suspicion. At times, I often repeated phrases, "No weapon forged against me shall prosper." If God's chosen people were to ride through this village, it'll have to be a theatrical stampede for glory. The Bible mentions an army of God in Revelation following a special someone. In respect to Tupac Amaru Shakur, about his mother, "You are appreciated." Marshal Eminem' Mather's, "I'm sorry Momma."

I partially couldn't understand why my mother stayed unprepared throughout some of this ordeal. She found it difficult to keep up with traditions as the illegal activity ran rampart, whereas no households seemed spared. We lived in an household nearly bankrupt with confusion, except for structural disciplinary action that had to be taken on my behalf. I never wanted to be a recipient of someone else's transgressions of betrayal, male nor female. A substandard conditioning from drugs, alcohol, and fornication should never been impressed upon me by the less privileged and underworking class poor with habitual personalities. My lack of formality materialized into organize chaos; a thought I never imagined where the ignorance seemed trending. The devastation of substance abuse impacted daily life on a scale far too dangerous for me to conceive.

I, personally and spiritually rather kept learning, for I sought alone. I became nomadic, resulting in learning Native American cultures. I spent a considerable amount of time amongst tribal elders gathering facts. The tribal nations I visited were the Choctaw, Cherokee, Lakota Sioux, just to name a few. I was once informed by my Lakota Sioux medicine man and spiritual guide to watch what I say about my mother. They valued family. It's perhaps something in women I recalled as a child that I rather search alone to destroy the abuse I witnessed growing up reigning in my mind as rage. If I never find it, Lord! Let me just keep my secondary education to myself.

The chronological changes to grow up becoming a young man perhaps came from seeing prominence in athletics, nothing more. In reminiscent with no support of my undefeated single season record in high school wrestling the year of 1989 was taken as luck with no recognition. I received no award in high school for such achievement, only in French. I felt someone would literally try and set me up and stability could not help me.

Needing help from prominent ladies and gentlemen in my life to stay busy and my identity destined for greatness were those too distracted by the overwhelming affects of crime and addiction. In the mist of this, I resorted to raise cats and stray dogs to guard the house where I resided.

Education during those times bored my family do the survival. The fast life of money was too irresistible and the focus wasn't being poor, by no means, but the might of the dollar in drug trafficking. Most of the males plummeted into the criminal justice system. The criminal element became acceptable, but not understandable. I informed my mother, either God is on our side or not and It's difficult to play both sides with regards to families immersed within worldly matters. This conversion became troubling sin in response to the need of responsibility. Crime sold and it was truly apparent along with dirty money. Faced being a Spiritual Prophetic Philosopher coded with the True Word of God was overshadowed as an acronym by overzealous peers.

I love my mother, but my quest for greatness was beyond comprehension of everyday life and my talents were somewhere else to be found. The strenuous siege was making it difficult to survive this new world order. Her southern hospitality slowly began to be of a past life experience and only a few existed from such a rich tradition.

For this reason, a quoted poem by Langston Hughes, called Cross: "My old man's a white old man and my old mother's black. If I ever cursed my white old man I take my curses back. If ever I cursed my black old mother and wished she where in hell, I'm sorry for that evil wish and now I wish her well. My old man died in the fine big house. My ma died in a shack. I wonder where I'm gonna die, Being neither white nor black?" (Langston Hughes)

I plan to never return here the way I'm departing. Many died because of ignorance in action. I witnessed many speeding to their graves by false intentions of subjecting themselves to the worship of engraving images, addiction, and greed. This lifestyle received so much news press than to even fathom the idea of stopping it can only kindle the flame.

Therefore, flirting with such crimes only proved ignorance in action, yet being well learned aided only towards moving onward in renaissance. I never really had close educated relations, do in part of criminalize participation, perhaps recalling mother-wit-sense with the remedy of wisdom from an elder. "Y'all kids are too bad to be so darn little." Granny chanted pointing onto me, "He shall raise up a nation that shall obey." I was inspired, yet fearful amongst the fray. Now, knowing what I know about families in peril, somehow I became in retrospect to Ralph Ellison's, The invisible man. I never wanted anyone to suffer. Oh Lord why, I? What I suffered was known as a mental breakdown and was hospitalized. I drew a timeline according to medical records; the evidence proves my case and legitimacy on what happened to my well-being. The melancholy from familial life lack one's social insight. This became mentally stressful causing nervous exhaustion. Sickness and fatalities where looked upon as a facetious object in one's life.

My greatness became asinine, and to the affect, Jesus Christ thought he was the son of God anointed with a crown made of thorns. Knowingly, Christ resurrected and ascended beyond the heavens through the sun. Christ as a man, during these present day times didn't save money, could not save himself and who gave a damn whether guns are loaded or not? The second coming to me, I must have a personal and spiritual relation, innately. "The fear of the Lord is the beginning of wisdom, but fools reject such knowledge and instructions." Out of all that glory coming down, I reduced it to a situation I knew that spoke symbolically. I still carry that pain, so what is redemption? I had already preconceive Christian teachings before I judged for myself, although my mind formulated its own opinion along a journey of perils.

The outsourcing of criminal behavior to feeble minds of substance abuse bled throughout the inner city. Would time tell or can they tell the times? A Subjection to weak inferior concepts, the path caused implosions within family structures. Huey P. Newton stated, "It's just family, also who da' daddy jokes." Insidious mingling has always pressured modern life. You know those who can't hide behind the painful truth. So, who will crown me, a person born in trouble sworn to secrecy? If I was on the run from law enforcement, it would be best for me not to have any family contacts. The life of sex, money, and murder would hinder any search to becoming a worthy manifested enlightened spirit, whereas resorting to the ballot or the bullet amongst guns and roses may not matter anymore.

Of all the male siblings of my brother and sisters, either they went to prison, or they've gotten killed. Surely, hell is not a badge of honor. I thought, we were raised better than having a jail house mentality, which is nothing to smile about. There is no cure for my bitterness for being civil. Lord, I beg thee, just allow this work-a-holic to migrate with the gifts I can conjure, because the hint of ignorance in action won't allow me to rest. Now, I'm a man and it would be best to hope and pray for them again, suffering from such mid-life crisis.

I use to think when times are hard, such as a recession, families should bond together, or maybe by clans. I wouldn't know from relatives who homes were already broken. Oh Lord! Who would want my demise? Why did they poison me? I tried to go somewhere and never be heard from again. The mental anguish of life from losing love ones had caused me to feel I'd gone crazy. A virtual Frankenstein living in fear resulted in me becoming an antisocial, eccentric, psychotic think tank, borrowing from all religions to find or create my own faith, for none here seemed enough to suit the rage of black indian trying to tame the devil's child, nigger savage trifling mentality. Knowingly, faith is something you have, not what you know. It's best for me never to talk of my familial crisis in regards to the penitentiary system or department of corrections. I would not know what it is anymore. My heart would fail that life, but never break it, therefore being the owner of a lonely heart is stronger. I'd seen many die-men-sons in East St. Louis. She meaning the mother earth deserves better.

I believe that schooling is the key towards social-economical peace when families are in turmoil. It measures and I don't think there is anything else to discuss, definitely when lewd inflammatory statements were constantly made in neighborhoods were it was everyday conversation. Never the less, disregarding my hall of records that lead me for decades. Meanwhile the conditions lacked community time management and had such an adverse effect on National Monuments and the environment (John Muir).

By identifying with historians (Sojourner Truth), Geniuses (Albert Einstein's General Relativity), Leaders (Former South Africa President, Nelson Mandela: The man that should have been my daddy. Movers and shakers are what my life was about the glorification of heavenly entities through writing, dance, and art then discussing the Word of God to making the world a better place with greatness (Desmond Tu Tu). When all is said and done, try fixing your face to figuring it out, by searching for yourselves. Little did we realize, "The true nature of a race is measured by the character of the woman, (Mary Mcleod Bethune)." So, when did we stopped being African Americans? All I know about family life were working minimum wage jobs and going to school just to pay bills.

For none attended any of my college events in sports and talent competitions. I even wrote a book my senior year in college. To my surprise of family and friends, if you can't match the splendor what an education bestowes, then your time had been wasted. As adults, we never took time to know one another's achievement or pursuits. Also,, no interest in my intellectual capabilities because they'd either stopped believing or dropped out of school and became accustomed to degradation. If kinship wasn't the natural way, then I believe in oneness. I love me and I learned as much as I can applying knowledge for the sake of living, "The Dream." The inner bliss is a path I know for certain, to communicate with the Heavenly Father, by utilizing solar energy to assist my seeing in dimensions. The fear of the Lord, and having greater responsibility for such gifted abilities to becoming a timeless oneness being.

I was forced to live a nomadic life which was my safety for a rare gift, by staying on the move and remain living aloof from family life, whereby the dirty dozen became ritual fact. Ridiculing the twelve tribes of Israel. Robbing Peter to pay Paul and watching Joe get lost. A sense of community urgency voiced by an individual's concern. Reminiscent to joseph in Genesis; it seems the story has been magnified in my favor without being incarcerated. Well, I became a stoic loner with special gifts, therefore I needed to concentrate on writing dance art solitaire avec mon le chamber de labatoire.

I had a hard time sustaining economic sufficiency; in and out of building maintenance and manufacturing jobs while learning and traveling abroad. I chose a college education, whether it spread sacredly, privately, and publicly. It meant everything; all or nothing. Throw me in the fray and I shall rise and succeed with flying colors. An honorary title, in my present day life was something of ancient times or when family values and status meant a purpose rooted in traditions. Now, disregarding whatever blessings or ideology maybe cursed and passed amongst individuals suffering from irresponsibility, instead of open-mindedness. One known fact, we never talked about strengthening the family with educational pursuits toward the "Middle-class" as this wise man remained a target.

A well-read human being that had so much to offer humanity, but my nerves damaged by events recalled by the decimation of a livelihood which were never compassionate throughout any of the ordeal. I, like the Post Mecca Malcolm X believe in intelligence is self defense and that violence can debunk God giving inalienable rights for human livelihood. "The use of the Proverbs is an exhortation to fear God and believe his word and to avoid the intentions of sinners."

I'd travel to many cities throughout the continental United States, embarking along life's journey with an education in creativity. Yet, I remained a bored drifting stranger, a lost shine, even in a place I once considered home. I only asked, but with doubt, if we ever see each other again, can we welcome in good spirits? I feel as though I don't know anymore, for wisdom is the equivalents of love. The two professors and a master of heavenly wisdom bestowed such a profound influence on the psyche. I prayed and now they are being answered.

God gave the Queen of England a Language that Angels can't sing. A curriculum I majored in college. I had two Brothers' whom shared the same ideology. Our solidarity merged an educational prophetic philosophy gained from our college professors, represent a candor rarely seen amongst mixed groups. I awaited the day to see them again.

The resemblance of my Brothers' eyes revealed a personal study of tracing and revealing a small portion 500 Nations of Indigenous roots. I awaited the day to see them again. My West African Brother and my American Brother who happens to be American white, teamed up with brothers' from multiple backgrounds.

Lifestyle of a god in my Brothers' eyes are our spiritual transparency. Our significance to this belief is not of ethnicity. Recalling the Post Mecca Malcolm X, were a friend gave one of Malcolm X's daughters two Barbie dolls. Meaning she was going to give her sister the other. If I'm not mistaken, he was a white guy. Malcolm X, walked over to the Barbie dolls to look at them, turns to his friend, and said? "I was too busy." When a man words can speak so profoundly as truth, in reality it doesn't match the words that he's use to speaking.

Aimless thoughts in my mind

danced along a whirling breeze,

at twilight time; spun leaves

shook from branched out trees,

earth toning the ground then freeze,

as the winds whistled;

summoned by fall shivering pleas.

CHAPTER III. BROTHERS'

Nearing winter of 1995, I visited two Brothers'. One in St. Louis, Missouri and the other in Southern Illinois whom were expert Analytical Thinkers and knew of my rare ability of seeing in dimensions. I had the honor amongst them to discuss the red, white, and blues. Since the United States were becoming either united or divided, we had to work diligently with expressiveness of English- speaking, figuratively. So, a phrase we established "God gave The Queen of England a Language that Angels can't sing." We were overwhelmed with a work load. The Post Industrial age dawned the informational and brought about the internet. Local, domestic, international, and universal information set the stage for the future media of education, entertainment, and intelligence, we dubbed edutainmentelligence. I saw within my Brothers' a God gene we shared without second guessing, therefore everything was suave. Our impression towards one another was genuine consistent flared laughter, no matter how we extended voraciously on the subject matter or level of communications, whereas the sarcasm gazed upon by on lookers seemed insane.

The historical literary events shared by the professor shaped our spiritual lives, never the less, bringing us together as Brothers' of the future manifested by the second coming. The seal of God on our foreheads revealed a lifestyle of a god in my Brothers' eyes. American men and women of the future. In my Brothers' eyes, I've foreseen expedition parallels of the Lewis and Clark expeditions accompanied by a Native American female guide name Sacajawea, and York, whom was a slave during those times. Without any realization, we had went full circle, whereby the lifestyle of a god yielded descendants of slaves, but according to my Brothers' eyes, these were not descendants of slaves. Yet, this Pre-Ecclesiastes oneness that was taken like a breath of fresh air.

The existence of (Hue)man beings. Whispering softly, simultaneously, "human beings, my brothers'." I replied, "Oh yeah! Human beings." Our ancestors declared, out of all the things that we've seen and went through, it does not define me, for there was no support, yet the wisdom was very alarming and made sure it was in concrete. The words they spoke were of divinity. I only recall the truth; telling no lie, yet I foreshadowed towards a distant future with the morality of divine guidance, because the constructs of a language to lead without reading a script (KRS1), is well defined in a Mother African tongue coded with The Queen's English. For all the Queens booties wear her colors. The exhortations chosen for those of priesthood and prince- hood; righteous duties granted onto having our purpose everywhere is a duty solemn of the creator regarding faith through spiritualism.

The perfect prime examples are W.E.B. Du Bois and Chief Joseph of the Nez Perce Indians, whom existed around the same time. "Lord, don't let my soul go down when Jesus is dead and God is gone (Soul of Black Folks, W.E.B. Dubois)." I wanted him to cure my soul and amp up my spirit. Instead he cured my spirit and amped up my soul. Of all the peace treaties established, not one was spared of being broken. Life itself yielded so much opposition. By the way, life doesn't require a few spare parts based on integrity, whereby these impressions while liquor, drugs, and soliciting set stationary at the helm of illegal activity. Subsequently, there are three choices for the Queen's English; standard, foreign, and broken for human beings in regions where the language was terribly broken. The vulgar usage of a language remains materialized into daily life. To my Brothers' eyes; never noticing it, but (English) was here, until divinity resulted in a plethora of intervention. God the Father, God the Son, and God the Great Holy Spirit, as I thought of the Queen's language of opportunity for purpose.

English, the proper pronunciation requires utilizing the stiff upper lip. Figuratively speaking, I stated we were living to see the snow on top. In other words, trying to grow old; becoming Elders not adversely tempted. So, when the questions about the gay community were asked, I reiterated on the question, you know; abruptly interrupting in regards to standing under an umbrella. By being astute to Inflammatory statements when threats on lives were acceptable to a means of proving valor as a pretense to parallel normal life. By nature, I was born free. Yet, the despise of others was where the language remained most potent. It spread throughout the city abnormalities amongst morals. Life executed a lot of changes, but it's not over. A once incarcerated soul briefly seeing the light, stated one said, a jail- house sissy had gay- dar; another false statement to judge an attack a fairer sex; trying to gain neighborhood publicity for criticizing and scapegoating me. I'd rather remain astute considering a human being's character reflective of one's on guilt. A puppet to the foolishness of social media platforms designed to misleading those with feeble minds.

A new thought in mind arrived for this new world order. The Str8, L, B, G, T, Q, may in a sense make reference to a wild ass of a man unscrupulous acts. By understanding the penitentiary definition of a pimp from judging the supreme law of the land to the politics across the land. The conspiracy of 2/3 to ¾ of a man by succubus, sodomy, adultery, amorphous, incest, pedophilia, and lust hungry cannibals with bestial behaviors of pagan heathens manipulation. Shipwrecked words with a row boat of thought, as the side affects of drugs such as heroine, crack, and amphetamines addiction causing poor judgment, ill will and withdrawal. From greed to misplaced trust and anxiety of losing out. It's like being caught up in God's four worlds of never finding reality, no matter what the season for inductive or deductive reasoning. With all the nonsense surrounding life itself, stems deceitful people with abnormal behaviors, as If they'd lost track of themselves from selling their fickle souls.

The window to souls in collaboration of conscious thought. I didn't mention the gay community whom build an economic base within civil unions. Vaguely, a piece of action for heterosexual black males are sublime to his on past of a rightful place and quickly blurred with feelings of being psychologically unrealistic. One will have to lose himself or herself to gender, as if a piece of action may already affected racial genders, except this constitutionality of rights granting orientation indiscriminate to never being considered equals, due to amended laws granted onto such group or groups. Monitoring actions and plans of surviving the ever changing working world's abused, by individuals living fully in this manner.

The heterosexual male may prove a false representation of his well being if keeping his sexuality private, perhaps sacred according to the opposite sex. A missed education maybe null and void, until the brainwashing of past lives resurrected by institutional depravity be transformed. Reluctantly, growing intellectually and finding a place too fitting, in this worldly sector may force a life of insecurities for deciphering one's on place of origin, perhaps the remittance of race to appeasing genders rigid towards a second hand emotion. The void of natural section in comparison to a host for like mindedness, or perhaps a relative of a kindred spirit.

There was a King in the Bible name David. David was a King of Jerusalem. His son, Solomon was known as the wisest man in the world. Before Solomon's birth, Dad had already laid the Foundation. A term which may seem to mimic what is a coach towards a fatherless child of finding his on way.

In reminiscent to legendary East Louis Sr. High School football coach released, due to politics of such insignificance. He has his wife and he's a winner. I occasionally chatted with coach during our championship times. He told me, "Jo, no matter what you do in life or be around; pay yourself first, because someone already paid the ultimate price for you." I thanked and honor him to this very day. "We as a people must show stubborn resilience in the face of adversity (President Obama)."

The advice from such individuals that's been in history books and athletics for generations, shall all ways be legendary to carry and spread as a reminder of the "American Dream" or at least I can say, the African Dream. Nothing should interfere with greatness, no matter the obstacles in the community. The str8, L, B, G, T, Q community does understand the great-nest in the arts. Although the arts of such communities are not of a cotton picker, bootlegger, and or sharecropper's profession to fairer sexes, perhaps it's a form of structuring within an all American nuclear family setting. The arts provided freedoms in personal liberties, but not the negative vices that plagues humanity. American injustice is too problematic for a gender friendly language to coexist or evolve throughout a turbulent society. The remedy is Jesus Christ!

Over consumption can psyche the mind, therefore too much study can weary the soul. The eyes are the window to the soul as everybody have their own opinions and views on dealing with ignorance. In San Francisco, there exist a cultural norm, whether a town meant for (edutainmentelligence), only when it comes to expression of the arts itself. Judging the behavior from where I am in a city lacking pity for unbalanced acts leading to funky booty dirty shit which is nothing more than a hard head toting a soft ass. Either turning-of-the-cheek, turning-the-others' cheek, turning up the cheek, or finally turning the other way. I was once known as a ho' town player during the expulsion of sugar daddies. I no longer have the desire. If my English were ever to be tainted, we will all be surprised in witness to god's wrath. In response to that, it's a thought because it's on how I viewed this. It's not my conclusion to only what I said, therefore it was just a thought.

A Choctaw Indian is not a cotton picker. Broken treaties infringing upon constitutionality, whether it's a ghetto or reservation. Young people should learn some history about their God given inalienable rights on righteousness and liberty. "It's just sprinkling words from a Queen, (Led Zeppelin)." When somebody break you off some proper English, don't shriek, just remain poised, then holla' be thou name. Is there a difference between a cotton picker in the south and a gang member of a housing apartment project? Start talking Southern country or Country southern hospitality, I can teach you Afrocentric American Humanitarianism, because ghetto greatness was inspired by all walks of life around the world. Uplifting the world's humanitarians are in the Will of God.

Hmmm! I know more in the air than in the ground. "Yes, my Brothers" I replied. "Yeah, Yah knows Choctaw." We can do anything in an era chosen for women. Ninety-nine problems and a chick ain't one, (Jay-Z). "Chi Kune Doe is broken rhythm which is better than a rehearsed routine, (Bruce Lee)." Yo! Gentlemen, we've gain immortality once again within the English language of tribal remedies, to an ancient Chinese secret for dance witnessing a soul seen by my Brothers' eyes. By focusing on your journey to judge ye not, for ye shall be judged. No matter where in the world we've find ourselves, we came to the same conclusion, God is real. By being on the watch for tormented souls, which is a solemn duty God bestowed onto me. The post Mecca Malcolm X and James Baldwin, The Fire Next Time for another day.

Tomorrow promises of sorrow
Only in a days life that follows,
For whom which It borrows;
fathoming melancholy so hollow
with filth made to wallow
In the dark shadows
Lurking amongst the gallows
where still waters not shallow,
but clearly a bitterness hard to swallow

CHAPTER IV. EYES

What is our world coming to? What is it that we've achieved in the past that's expected from an American people's future? Where is the honor for loving the consistency of greatness? Is there a difference between human beings, whereby our ethical ethos coincide with our insecurities. I'd worked very hard to stay busy in the world's oldest profession, than to not exist in a place where I am needed. Average people may rarely think of soul searching as for as the sweet pleasures of youth remain occupying their lives. From the absence of balance, I became a weary soul, however, I stressed "emotional content, not anger, (Bruce Lee)." I am strong and mastered my existence as well as my experience and came to a full circle in life. I'd even forgiven the trespassers. For all of those who impeded life greatest aspirations; the immoral acts that are inadvisable may be considered acceptable, but not understandable; shall be caught off guard within the sins of free will.

God grants a serenity, in acceptance for the things that cannot change, yet courage in changing the things possible, plus wisdom to making a difference. How to get people to think and see clearly to understand and come to a conclusion in perspective towards changing minds. American street blacks whom lack experience with the English language, making a market of mockery for black on black crimes and welcoming a down-hill pull; trying to find better ways to destroy themselves and not taking anything with it. Action figures, each sold separately; sold in and sold out of responsibility of life's values. The suffering from the lack of livelihood.. The need to comprehend the irresponsibility of family values being a racist code word. That's if you are unaware of the vices that plagues humanity. There's always room for disciplinary action, no matter the ethnicity, as long as the merit for changing minds meet the requirement to think in position of influence.

Therefore, in conclusion, I came to the realization that I am a valuable thought. There were those in the past who told me that I won't mount to much. I went and asked black and white folks in favor of changes to making communities prosper and thrive better. They stated, "G-E-T Y-O-U-R E-D-U-C-A-T-I-O-N!" I'd given my life to the English Language historically and someday return to an American way of living, for a movement that's financially sustainable. A timeless oneness being driven inward recalled my genetic code in regards to a life beginning again, in observance of falling spirits to lost souls.

Eventually, an exodus from all things witnessed. By casting oneself as a minor god in my Brothers' eyes represents the imagination of the gifts bestowed upon me by the creator. A celestial prophet with an extraterrestrial ability for seeing in dimensions, similar to Edgar Casey, known as the sleeping prophet. The same concepts stated about an education, amen. My grandmother constantly warned me about my education, but now I see myself as omniscient to engraving foreshadowed vents.

Joseph was known as a visionary, the decoder of dreams in the Bible. Joseph was also second in charge to the King of Egypt when he wasn't on the throne. The dreamer of dreams, yet mine became a reality. The parallels are frightening, as much as they are good.

So, Please! When learning Queen Elisabeth II English; if you don't understand, c'est la vie. When it comes to a language, there is an order. If you don't know yourself from a hole in the ground, then study English. Whatever it did to me, maybe the English language can do the same thing for you. Peace!

A Spiritual Prophetic Philosophy for Humanitarian Purposes in Religious and Cultural Philanthropy. Be Real Open To Hearing Existing Reality, and Search Inner-Self to Every Reason; the Honor of Our Dreams, of Having Our Purpose Everywhere, by Cornelius Joseph.

BIOGRAPHY

Joseph Allen is from East Saint Louis, Illinois. While in high school, Joe set an undefeated single season record in Greco-Roman freestyle wrestling, qualifying for the Illinois state championships. After graduating from high school in 1989, he attended Blackburn College, earning a B.A. degree in written communications. Throughout his college career, he played basketball, participated in a talent show and winning a dance group competition. He wrote for the Vortex, a literary magazine that's published yearly. This is where he gained potential insight for having a gift in writing on intriguing topics and ideas. Many of Joe's talents stem from creative writing, phenomenal dance, and spiritual art. He enjoys traveling and exploring different cultures as a means of broadening one's horizon. By grasping a code of many colors through diversity, he realizes a Renaissance taking shape within American society. The study of liberal arts originated an Enlightened within his writing for Renaissance. Joseph is currently working in the residential construction field rehabbing houses. During Joe's spare time away from work, he exercises to maintaining physical shape geared for enduring times of chronological changes.